PEOPLE WHO HELP US

TEACHER

Rebecca Hunter

Photography by Chris Fairclough

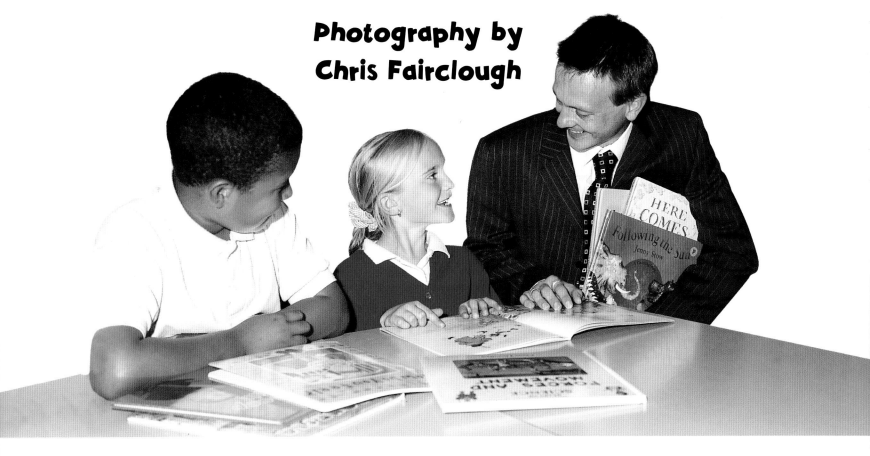

CHERRYTREE BOOKS

A Cherrytree book

First published in 2005 by
Evans Brothers Ltd
2A Portman Mansions
Chiltern Street
London W1U 6NR

British Library Cataloguing in Publication Data
Hunter, Rebecca
  Teacher. – (people who help us)
    1. Teachers – Juvenile literature
    I. Title
    371.1

ISBN 1842343009

Planned and produced by Discovery Books Ltd
Editor: Rebecca Hunter
Designer: Ian Winton

Acknowledgements
Commissioned photography by Chris Fairclough.

The author, packager and publisher would like to thank the following people for their participation in the book: Paul Hargreaves, Ken Kies and the staff and pupils of Runwell Primary School, Essex.

Words appearing in bold **like this**, are explained in the glossary.

Contents

I am a teacher

My name is Paul. I am a **teacher**.

This is the school where I teach.
It is called Runwell Primary
School and
is in Essex.

8.00 I arrive at school in my car.

Our school is not very large. It has 300 **pupils** and 12 full-time teachers.

A maths lesson

The first lesson today is maths with Year Three.
The pupils are learning to tell the time.

I write down a time of day on a piece of paper.
The children have to move the hands of the
clock on the **whiteboard** to the correct time.

Then the children do some written work about time and clocks. Adam has finished his work. He asks me to check if he has got it right.

Breaktime

10.30 Time for break. It is my turn to be on playground **duty**. I **supervise** the children while they play. Our school has an **assault course**.

This is Lucy on the climbing frame.

And here is Frazer balancing on the beam. They must both be careful not to fall off!

The teacher on duty makes sure the children are safe and happy. Some children tease others, sometimes there can even be bullying.

The children know they can talk to me if anything bad is happening.

Time for games

Today in games, we are going to practise some events for sports day.

First we do some warming up exercises.

Then we play a game with the ball.

The children are doing running races. They are divided into boys' and girls' **heats**.

I blow the whistle to tell them when to start.

Lunch

12.30 Time for lunch. On sunny days some teachers like to eat outside. I join Ms Blandford, one of the other teachers, at the garden table.

These children have brought packed lunches to school.

Most of the children have lunch in the dining room. Today they are having fish fingers and jelly.

Lunchtime is supervised by the dinner ladies. They help cut up the food of the smaller children.

13

Staff meeting

While the children are having their lunch, I have a **staff** meeting with Mr Kies, the headteacher, and Ms Blandford. We discuss next week's school concert. Rhian, the school **secretary**, takes down the notes.

After the staff meeting I change out of my games clothes and make a cup of coffee in the staff room.

Then I sit down at my laptop computer.
I often use the Internet to research and prepare my lessons.

The library

It is **literacy** hour and we are using the library. Lalita is a library **monitor**. She is helping William take out a book. She scans the book's **bar code** with the computer **scanner**.

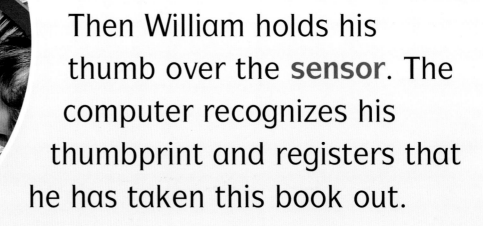

Then William holds his thumb over the **sensor**. The computer recognizes his thumbprint and registers that he has taken this book out.

Jade chooses a book from the book corner.

Then she joins Ben who is her **book buddy**. He listens to her read, and helps her with difficult words.

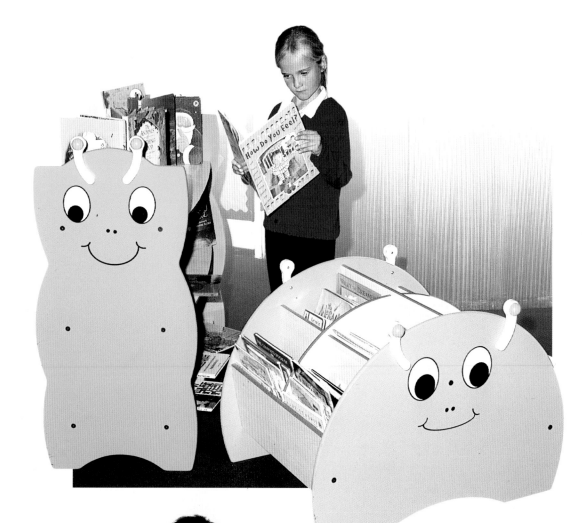

I ask Jade questions about the story.

Art class

Now I have an art class with Year One. They are making life-size pictures of people. The children lie down on large pieces of paper. Then I help them draw around each other.

Next the children paint in the outlines.

I hang the paintings up to dry.

When they are dry we cut them out.

Oscar has painted his picture to look like himself. It is a life-size **self-portrait**!

Time to go home

At the end of the day I help Mr Kies with a singing **rehearsal** for the school concert.

He plays the guitar and the children practise their songs.

3.15 Time to go home.
The parents collect their
children at the school door.

I tell the parents what
we have done today
and say goodbye to
the children.

After school

Although school is over, my day is not finished yet. I run an after-school tennis club with some of the older children.

Then I will go home and prepare some work for tomorrow.

Next week I am going on a **first-aid** course. A **supply teacher** will cover for me.

Being a teacher is hard work but lots of fun!

Glossary

assault course a set of different types of exercise equipment

bar code a pattern of lines and numbers that can be read by a computer

book buddy an older child who helps a younger one with his or her reading

duty something someone does as part of his or her job

first-aid the treatment given to a person who is injured or feeling ill

heats separate rounds in a competition that decide who will compete in the final

literacy the ability to read and write

monitor a pupil who is chosen to do special tasks

pupils the children who attend a school

rehearsal a practice of a play or concert or other event

scanner a machine that is used to examine something by moving a beam of light over it

secretary a person who works in an office; he or she keeps records and writes letters

self-portrait a picture of a person drawn by himself/herself

sensor a piece of equipment that can identify what something is

staff the people who work for an organization

supervise to be in charge of people

supply teacher a teacher who stands in when another teacher is away from school

teacher someone who teaches at a school or college

whiteboard an electronic classroom board that can display information from a computer

Index